Music Help

by Lilly Cho
illustrated by Kristen Goeters

Practice Decodable 56

McGraw Hill Education

Bothell, WA • Chicago, IL • Columbus, OH • New York, NY

MHEonline.com

Send all inquiries to:
McGraw-Hill Education
8787 Orion Place
Columbus, OH 43240

ISBN: 978-0-02-138967-4
MHID: 0-02-138967-5

Printed in China.

8 9 10 11 12 DSS 27 26 25 24 23

"Smoke harmed things," whispered Mom.
"The Joneses can use a little help."

That made Matt think.

Dad gave music lessons.

Dad and his pupils had a band.
They made music for fun.

"Dad's band can make music," said Matt.
"We can collect cash to help the Joneses!"

Dad's band had a concert.
Matt sang a cute song.

The concert was a huge success.
After the concert, Mr. Jones thanked Matt.